The Lie

Peter Leigh

JAMESTOWN PUBLISHERS

a division of NTC/CONTEMPORARY PUBLISHING GROUP

Lincolnwood, Illinois USA

First published in United Kingdom by Hodder & Stoughton
Educational in Association with the Basic Skills Agency.

ISBN: 0-89061-624-8

Published by Jamestown Publishers,
a division of NTC/Contemporary Publishing Group, Inc.
4255 West Touhy Avenue,
Lincolnwood (Chicago), Illinois 60646–1975 U.S.A.
© 1998 by NTC/Contemporary Publishing Group, Inc.
Manufactured in the United States of America.

890 V P 0 9 8 7 6 5 4 3 2 1

KALEIDOSCOPE

The Lie

Contents

1

Class Pest

Luke hated Mr. Jones.
From the first time he saw him he hated him.

He hated the way he said,
"Hi, my name's Bob Jones.
I'm your new teacher."
He hated the way the class said,
"Hi, Mr. Jones!" back.
He hated his little ponytail.
He hated the way he smiled at the girls,
and the girls smiled at him.

He hated the way the boys talked about
football to him,
and told him about their best games.
He hated him because he taught religious education.
Religious education was a stupid subject.
But most of all he hated Mr. Jones
because Miss Smith liked him.
And Luke liked Miss Smith.

Miss Smith was their new math teacher
who had come last term.
She was young and pretty.
Luke used to leer at her from his desk.

"Come and show us how you multiply, Miss,"
he would say.
"I like a little multiplying."

Once he said a very rude word.

"Luke!" said Miss Smith.

"Sorry, Miss," said Luke.
"It just slipped out.
It often slips out.
I can't help it."

When Mr. Jones arrived,
he and Miss Smith were often seen together,
on duty or in the library.
And Miss Smith kept coming into
Mr. Jones' classroom
to borrow an eraser or a piece of chalk.
The girls looked at one another and giggled.
Luke looked from Miss Smith, to the girls,
and then to Mr. Jones.

That was when Luke decided it was war.

Mr. Jones always tried to make the lessons
interesting.
Luke always tried to ruin them.

"We don't want to do this.
This is boring," he said.

"We want to do interesting work."

"This is interesting," said Mr. Jones,
"if you tried."

"No, it's not. It's boring."

Luke said this every lesson.

Mr. Jones brought in a video.
"I'll do it," said Luke
before Mr. Jones could stop him.
He jammed the tape.
"That video is useless," said Luke.

A group of girls was using the computer.
"It's my turn," said Luke.
"Let me go. It's not fair. You always let the girls
go first."

The girls looked at one another.
They knew Luke.
"Let him have a turn, sir," said one of them.

KALEIDOSCOPE

"It will be quicker in the end."

Luke banged his hands down on the keys
and broke the mouse.
"This computer is garbage," he said.

Wherever Mr. Jones wanted him to sit,
Luke wanted to move.
Whoever he had to sit next to,
he wanted to sit next to someone else.
He never had a pen, or a pencil, or his book.
And it was always someone else's fault.

"It's not my fault!" he would say.
"You're picking on me.
You're always picking on me.
It's not me. It's the others.
Don't blame me."

And he always knew exactly how far to go.

When Mr. Jones was talking to boys about a
football game, Luke said,
"You like boys, don't you, sir!"

Mr. Jones looked at him hard.

"What do you mean by that, Luke?"

"Well, you like talking to boys.

About football I mean.

I expect you like watching them as well."

Once he said to Ashok, a fellow Pakistani student,

"Give us your eraser, you Paki!"

and Ashok tried to punch him.

"Oh, sir!" cried Luke.

"He's hitting me! Sir, he's hitting me,

and I didn't do nothing!"

"He called me a Paki," said Ashok.

"Oh, no, I didn't, sir! That's racist!

I wouldn't say that!

He's lying.

He's just trying to get me into trouble!"

And Mr. Jones looked from Luke to Ashok
and back to Luke.

When Mr. Jones told Gary off
for not having a pen,
Luke said, "Don't blame him, sir.
It's not his fault. It's his mom!"

Mr. Jones had to hold Gary back.

"What's the matter?" said Luke,
"I didn't say nothing. I was trying to help!"

When Laura finished her drawing of a temple,
which had taken her all lesson,
Luke walked past her desk.
He tripped and spilt ink all over it.
"Oh, what a shame," he said.
"After you spent so long on it as well.
It was just an accident."

2

2

KALEIDOSCOPE

"Stupid Luke"

It was the last lesson before lunch.
The class was doing posters
of famous sayings from the Bible—
"Do unto others as you would be done to,"
"Blessed are the peace-makers,"
and *"Pride goes before a fall."*

Luke had done nothing.
He had spent the lesson flicking pellets.
He had caught Laura behind the ear.

8

She started to cry.

"Don't look at me," he said
when Mr. Jones tried to find out
what happened.
"It wasn't me!"

Mr. Jones looked at the smudged, torn piece of
paper on Luke's desk.

"You haven't done anything, Luke.
You haven't even opened your book.
At least look as though you have done
something."

Luke opened the Bible on his desk.
He flipped over the pages.

"Here, sir," he said.
"I'm in the Bible.
Page after page of me.
I'm a saint. Saint Luke."

"Yes, Luke," said Mr. Jones.
"Your name.
But that's the only thing
you have in common with Saint Luke."

Luke started to read,
Forasmuch—as—many—have—
taken—in—hand
. . . What? . . .
in—hand—to—set—forth—in—order . . .
What's this?
. . . in—order—a— declaration—of . . ."

Luke threw the Bible down.
"This is garbage.
This Saint Luke is stupid."

"Oh, I was wrong," said Mr. Jones.
"Two things in common!"

It wasn't very funny.
It wasn't meant to be very funny.
But the class wanted to laugh,
and they wanted to laugh at Luke.

They howled, and they roared,
they pointed at him,
and they banged their desks.

The bell rang.
"Off you go to lunch," said Mr. Jones,
and the class went out still laughing.

Luke was not laughing.
There was a cold fury inside him,
and only he noticed
that as Mr. Jones left, smiling to himself,
he forgot to lock the classroom door!

3

Revenge

Luke closed the door quickly behind him.

The room was empty.

The corridor outside had been empty too.

He looked around.

What could he do?

Something to pay back that Mr. Jones,

teach him not to make fun of him.

And those stupid kids.

They'll learn not to laugh at him.

He'll show them.

His eyes flew around the room.

Where?
What?

And then he saw the pile of posters on
Mr. Jones' desk
that the class had been working on.
Luke smiled.
This was going to be easy.

He glided across the room
and picked up the posters.
Some of them had already been pinned up
by Mr. Jones.
Luke looked through the others.
They were all carefully drawn and colored:
"Goody-goodies!" said Luke to himself,
"sucking up to the teacher."

Angrily he threw them onto the floor.

On the desk was a bottle of ink
and a plastic bottle of glue.
Luke grinned.
He'd show them.

He unscrewed the top off the glue bottle
and laid it on the edge of the desk.
The glue oozed out
and fell in a long stream on the posters below.
Quickly he did the same with the bottle of ink.

He watched the glue and ink
spread thickly over the class's work.
Luke was well pleased.

There was no time to waste now.
He flew over to the door,
grinning to himself
at the thought of Mr. Jones' face
when he found the mess.

4

Anger

He opened the door and gasped.

Mr. Jones was standing there.

He looked as surprised as Luke,

as if he was about to open the door

from the other side.

"Luke?" he said.

"What are you doing here?"

Luke said nothing.

He peered around Mr. Jones
looking for a way out.
There was no way out.
Mr. Jones was blocking the whole doorway.

"I asked you a question, Luke.
What are you doing here?"

"Nothing!
I'm not doing nothing!
I . . . I heard a noise,
and . . . and I came in to check."

"What?
You heard a noise?
You don't expect me to believe that."

He came forward,
forcing Luke back into the room,
and closed the door behind him.

"You were stealing things, weren't you?
Books, pens, paper,
anything you could get your hands on."

"I was not!
I tell you, I was going past the door,
and I heard a noise."

"Nonsense!
What noise?
And what were you doing here
in the first place?
You should be outside!"

"I . . . I was looking for you!
To explain.
About the Bible.
I didn't understand,
and I was looking for you to explain!"

"Don't give me that!
The door was open,
and you thought you'd . . . you'd . . ."

Mr. Jones' voice trailed off.

He went very pale,
and his mouth dropped open.
He had seen the mess on the floor.

"I heard a noise,
and I came in," said Luke.
"Then I saw that mess,
so I was coming to report it to you.
Right away!"

Mr. Jones didn't say anything.

Luke looked at Mr. Jones' face
with his mouth still hanging open.
He started to giggle.
Mr. Jones looked really stupid.

"It's a real mess, isn't it?
The class will be really upset.
All that work.
Someone doesn't like you!"

Mr. Jones turned towards Luke.

His face was pale,
and he was trembling.

"You little jerk!" he said.

Luke was shocked.

"You shouldn't say that," he said.
"Teachers shouldn't use bad words.
It's against the law!"

Mr. Jones said it again.
"You little jerk!"

He came closer.
His eyes were icy,
and his voice was low.

"You've done this, haven't you!
You're sick.
Do you know that?
You're sick."

"You shouldn't say that.
I'll tell on you,
saying that, you . . . OW!"

Luke felt a sudden, sharp pain on his ear.
Mr. Jones had hit him!
Luke was more surprised than hurt.
Mr. Jones had hit him!

"You shouldn't do that.
It's against the law! OW!"

Mr. Jones had hit him again!
And again!

But now Luke was angry.
He lashed out with his fist and his boot,
but Mr. Jones held him at arm's length with one
hand, and slapped him across the face
with the other.

Luke squealed and shouted,
and kicked and punched.

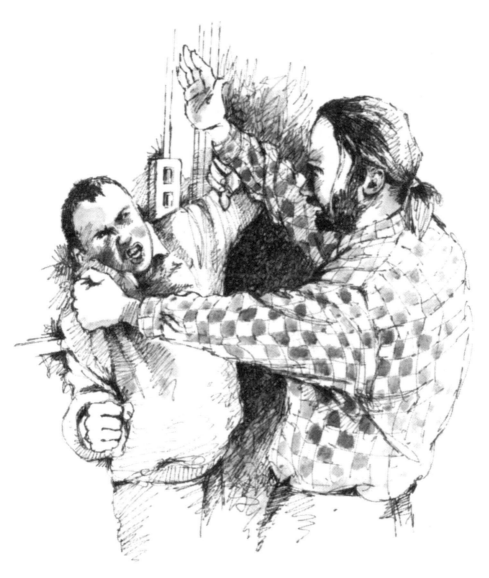

But it was no good.

Backwards and forwards went Mr. Jones' hand.

Smack! Smack! Smack!

22

And at the same time he swore at Luke
in a low and nasty voice.

Luke broke free
and staggered to the door.
He was gasping for breath.
He had been half choked by Mr. Jones.
His face was stinging with pain.
He wrenched the door open
and turned around.

Mr. Jones was standing
in the middle of the room.
His hair had come out of the ponytail,
and his face was red.
He was panting.
Luke was shaking with anger.
He glared at Mr. Jones.

"I'll get you for this!" he hissed.
"I'll get you so bad!
I'll get my dad on to you!
I'll get the law on to you!

KALEIDOSCOPE

I'll get you fired!
In prison!
You can't hit kids.
It's against the law.
You're finished! You hear me? You're . . ."

Mr. Jones lunged at him.
But Luke darted through the doorway
and ran down the corridor.
At the end he turned again and screamed,
"I'll get you.
You see if I don't!"
And then he ran through the main door,
out into the yard.

It was the end of lunch.
Luke shouted,
"Jones has beat me up! Jones has beat me up!"

Everyone turned to look.

Luke shouted again,
"Jones has beat me up!

24

I'm getting the police!
He beat me up."

From all over the school kids started to run
towards him.
Luke shouted it again and again,
and a crowd gathered around him.
The kids' faces were excited
and a little frightened.
He pushed his way through shouting,
"I'm going to get him! I'm going to get him!"
When he got to the gates, he yelled,
"I'm getting the police, NOW!"

And then he ran out.
Behind him he could hear the crowd buzzing—
"Luke . . . beaten up . . . Mr. Jones . . .
the police . . . prison!"

5

War

Luke's dad was slumped
in front of the television.
He had a can of beer in his hand.
He was muttering to himself.

"Darned television!
Nothing on!
There never is!
They never put anything good on!"

He had just got off shift.
The only thing he could do was sit.
He was too tired for anything else.

"You work your guts out,
and what do you get for it?
A few, miserable dollars!
So you put the TV on for a bit of
entertainment, and what is there?
Nothing!
There never is! They never put
anything good on . . ."

The front door crashed open,
and Luke came running in.

"What are you doing home at this time?"

"They beat me up at school, Dad!
The teachers!
That Mr. Jones! He did it!
He beat me up for no reason!"

"What?

What are you talking about?"

Luke told him again.
"That Mr. Jones!
He slapped me across the face!
Again and again!
And I didn't do nothing!
He hit me for no reason!
And he swore at me!
He's always picking on me!"

"What?"

Luke had to go through it three times,
before it finally sunk in.
But by the time he had finished
for the third time,
Luke could see his dad was angry,
really angry.
All his tiredness was gone.

They were at it again, weren't they?
Picking on his Luke,
just like they picked on him.

Well, he wasn't having it!
Not by a long way!
And if they thought he was,
then they've got another thought coming!

"Listen to me, son!
We'll get them, don't worry!
We're going back to that school now,
and we're going to get the law on them.
They think they can walk all over us,
but they can't,
and they're going to find out they can't.
We'll get that Mr. Jones!
We'll get him fired,
and see if he likes it on the dole!"

He snatched up the phone
and stabbed out a number with his finger.

"Is that the police?
Listen, you better get down to the school,
right away.

My boy Luke has been beaten up
by one of the teachers. Mr. Jones.
He smashed his face in.
The boy can hardly talk.
It's assault!
I'm going down there now.
I'm going to get him.
You better be there,
otherwise there will be murder.
I won't be responsible!"

He slammed the phone down.

"Come on, Luke. We'll make them pay!"

He grabbed Luke and strode out of the house.

6

Serious Charges

When they got to the school,
there was a police car parked outside.
It was empty.

Luke's dad marched past it
with Luke just behind him.

They went through the gates,
between the buildings and then
in the main door.

They marched along the corridor.

And as they marched
Luke could hear the kids behind him,
rushing to the windows and the doors,
and the teachers trying to stop them
and get them back to their seats.

Luke felt great!
The whole school was buzzing!
They all knew what had happened.

They all wanted to see
what he was going to do about it!

Him!
Luke!

His chest swelled,
and he glowed.
He had forgotten the pain in his ear.
In fact he looked really cheerful.

They came to the principal's office.

"You can't go in there!" said a secretary.
"You have to wait and . . ."
Luke's dad brushed her aside.
He didn't even knock on the door.
He marched straight in with Luke behind him.
The principal was standing by her desk
talking to a policeman.

"I want him fired," said Luke's dad,
so that the whole school could hear.

"I want him fired,
and I want him fired now!"

"Ah, yes, Mr. . . ."
said the principal trying to close the door
behind him.
"If you would come in and sit down . . ."

I want that Jones!
I want him fired!
I want him behind bars!
Do you hear me?"

"Yes, I do hear you, Mr. . . .
Perhaps if you were to come in and . . ."

"He hit my son.
That's against the law,
and I want him fired."

"Yes, I know.
But these are serious charges,
and we have to . . . to . . .

Perhaps you would like a cup of tea," she said.

"Tea? I don't want tea!
I want him fired!
Understand?
Fired!"

"Yes, of course! I'm sorry!
Look, I have already sent for Mr. Jones.
The police are here, and I promise you
we will get to the bottom of it,
but you must come in and sit down."

Luke's dad calmed down
and sat down.
Luke sat next to him.

"Let's just wait till Mr. Jones gets here,
shall we?" said the principal.

She went back behind her desk and sat down.
The policeman sat next to her.
They all sat and waited quietly.

For a long time.

At last there was a soft knock on the door.

"Come in," said the principal.
The door opened.
Mr. Jones came in.

He had washed
and combed his hair back into the ponytail,
but his face was still a little pale.

"You wanted to see me?"
He sounded interested,
but a little puzzled
as if he had no idea what this was all about.

"Yes, Mr. Jones. Sit down please."

Mr. Jones sat down.

"Now, Mr. Jones,
there have been some very serious charges
made against you."

"Against me?"
He sounded shocked.

"Yes, I'm afraid so.
These charges are so serious
that the police are here as well.
Now, in a moment I'm going to ask Luke
to tell us exactly what happened this morning.
Is that all right?"

She looked at Luke's dad,
and he nodded.

She looked at the policeman,
and he nodded.

Then she turned to Luke.
She smiled gently.
"Now Luke," she said.
"I know this is going to be difficult for you,

but I want you to be brave.
Will you be brave for me Luke?"

Luke nodded.

"There's a good boy.
Now Luke,
I want you to stand up in front of me and
these gentlemen, and tell us exactly what
happened this morning.
Can you do that Luke?"

"I'll try," said Luke weakly.

"Good boy," said the principal again.

Luke stood up.
He looked hurt, and a little sad.

"It all started in the lesson this morning.
I didn't understand what we were supposed to do.
I didn't understand
because Mr. Jones was picking on me.

He was picking on me all the lesson.

He was making a joke about my name.

He always picks on me.

It's because I'm not as clever as the others

and that's why he picks on me.

He doesn't pick on the others

especially the girls.

He likes the girls.

He always gives them high marks,

and he never picks on them.

But I do try.
Really I do. Ever so hard!
And that's why I was looking for
Mr. Jones at lunch.
So he could explain the work again.
Well, I went to knock on his door,
when I heard this noise inside.
So I thought, that must be Mr. Jones.
So I open the door and go in.
But there's no one there.
So I turn around to go out again,
when I see this big mess on the floor.
'Oh, no!' I said.
'Mr. Jones will be ever so upset.
I must report it right away!'
I turn around to go out
when in comes Mr. Jones.
He starts on at me, saying
I'm stealing things.
'No, I'm not!' I said,
but he doesn't listen. He never listens.
I try to explain,
but he keeps on and on at me—

'You're stealing things! You're stealing things!'
'I'm not!' I said.
But it don't make no difference.
And then he sees the mess.
And he starts swearing at me.
Oh, miss,"—

Luke paused and looked straight at the principal—

"he was swearing some terrible words.
And then he grabs me,
and starts hitting me,
and he doesn't stop,
and I'm shouting
'Please, sir! Stop!
Oh you're hurting me! Please, sir!',
but he doesn't take any notice.
He just keeps on hitting me,
again and again,
hitting me,
and it hurts, and the pain,
oh, my head,
it's awful,

the pain . . .
the pain . . ."

Luke put his head in his hands and cried.
Luke's dad jumped up
and put his arms around Luke.

"There now son.
It's all right now.
It's all right now!"

"Yes, Luke," said the principal.
"It's all right now.
I think we can guess the rest.
Sit down
and you'll feel better in a minute."

Luke's dad was pointing at Mr. Jones.
"You see what he's done.
Hitting kids.
That's battery, that is! Assault and battery!
I want him put away!
I want him locked up!"

"Yes, yes! Please, sit down!"
said the principal.

Luke sat down with his dad.
He still had his head in his hands,
but he listened very carefully.

Inside he was crowing!

7

Trapped

"Well, Mr. Jones," said the principal.
"You've heard what Luke has had to say.
What do you have to say?"

Mr. Jones sat silently.
He did not move.
He seemed deep in thought.

The silence went on and on.

"Well?" said the principal.

Finally, Mr. Jones raised his head.

"I don't know where to begin," he said.
"Because, you see,
every word that Luke has said is a lie!
Every single word!"

Luke's dad jumped up.
"What?
Are you calling my son a liar?
That's libel!
I'll get you for that. I'll . . ."
He went to hit Mr. Jones
and had to be held back by the policeman.

"Sit down, please, sit down," said the principal.

Luke's dad was calmed down.

"Continue please, Mr. Jones."

"Yes! I'm sorry to say it,
but Luke is lying.
I did not swear at Luke.
I did not take hold of Luke.
I did not hit Luke.
All of that is a total lie!
Because you see,
I could not have done these things,
even if I had wanted to,
because at the time when
Luke says they happened
I was out of school.
I have been out of school for the whole lunch.
In fact, this is the first time I have seen Luke,
since the lesson this morning."

Luke gasped.
He stared at Mr. Jones.
"But . . . But . . ." he tried to say,
but the words would not come.
His ears could not believe
what they had heard.
Mr. Jones had lied!

The policeman was talking.
It was the first time he had spoken.

"Let me get this straight, Mr. Jones.
Do you deny all of this?"

"Yes!"

"You never swore at Luke?"

"No!"

"You never grabbed him?"

"No!"

"And you never hit him?"

"No! Most certainly not!
I would never dream of doing such a thing.
It goes against everything I believe in,
everything I stand for."

He looked at the principal.
"I think that children who are already victims
shouldn't be victims of school as well,
that children who are hurt by society
shouldn't be hurt by teachers."

The principal nodded wisely.
The policeman went on.

"And you were nowhere near school all lunch?"

"No, I was not!"

"Where were you then?"
"I was walking nearby.
There's some lovely countryside
near the school.
Teaching is very stressful, you know,
and I find walking very relaxing."

"Was there anyone with you?
Anyone who saw you?

Anyone who could support your story?"

"Yes, there was!"

Mr. Jones paused, looked at Luke,
and then said clearly,
"Someone who was with me the whole time.
Someone who can support
every word I have said.
I was with Joanne.
That is, Miss Smith."

He smiled shyly at the principal.
"As you might have heard,
Miss Smith and I have been seeing
a lot of each other recently,
and we often spend lunch together."

"Miss Smith?" said the policeman,
looking towards the principal,
but she was already tapping out a number
on her phone.

"Miss Smith please . . . Yes, it's the principal."

There was a pause.

"Ah, Miss Smith.
Can you tell me please,
where were you this lunchtime?
. . . Right! Yes!
And tell me, and this is very important,
was anyone with you?
. . . Right!
And was that for the whole lunchtime?
. . . Right!
I see! Thank you very much Miss Smith.
That will be all."

The principal put the phone down and looked up.

"Miss Smith says she was walking
in the country for the whole lunchtime
with Mr. Jones!"

At last Luke found his voice.

"It's a lie," he shouted. "It's all lies.
He beat me up. He hit me.
Ask anyone."

"Who?" said the policeman.
"Who shall I ask?
Who saw it, Luke?
Who are the witnesses?"

"But . . . but . . ." but there was no one.
He had told lots of kids,
but no one had actually seen it.
"But . . . but . . . he's lying.
They're both lying."

"Are you saying that two of your teachers
are lying?"

"Yes . . . he's picking on me again . . .
it's because of the mess in his room . . .
he's picking on me."

"And that's another thing,"

Mr. Jones spoke again.
"Luke said that he went into my room at lunch
and found a mess on the floor. Right?"

Everyone nodded.

"Well, Luke is quite right.
I have just been to my room
and there is a mess on the floor,
a horrible mess.
Now seeing as I was out of school
the whole lunch,
and seeing as Luke himself says
he went in my room,
then the only person who could have made
the mess is Luke.
So, he wrecked my room
and made up this whole story
to get himself out of trouble!"

Luke jumped up.

"No! That's not right."

52

There was something wrong
about what Mr. Jones said,
but Luke couldn't quite work out what it was.
He started to object,
but suddenly there was another stinging pain
on his ear.

"You little liar," shouted his dad,
smacking him around the head.
"Getting me down here for nothing!
You wait till I get you . . ."

Now it was just one big quarrel.
Luke shouted and screamed and struggled
with his dad.
His dad shouted at Luke
and tried to hit him.
The policeman shouted at both of them
and tried to separate them.
And the principal told everybody to sit down.

The only one who was quiet was Mr. Jones.
He sat watching it all.

Finally, the policeman pulled Luke's dad off.
"You wait till I get you home,"
he was shouting.
"You just wait!"
The policeman took him out through the door.
They could still hear him shouting
down the corridor.

The principal turned to Mr. Jones.
"I don't think we need to keep you any longer,
Mr. Jones.
Thank you," he said.

He got up and walked towards the door.
But as he reached it he turned.

"Please don't be too hard on Luke!" he said.
"He needs help, not punishment."
And then he went out.

The principal turned and looked at Luke.
"Sit down, Luke," she said.

It's Not Fair!

Luke sat in a classroom by himself.

His mind was whirling.

It was the classroom that Mr. Jones had taught

them in that morning.

Some of the posters were pinned up

on the wall.

The principal had put him there

while she decided what to do with him.

He might be suspended.

That didn't worry Luke.
It was a few days off school.

He might get a beating from his dad.
That didn't worry him either.
He had had beatings before,
and knowing his dad
he might well have forgotten all about it
by the time he got home.

No, it wasn't that Luke was thinking about.
It was Mr. Jones!
He had lied!

Luke couldn't get it out of his head.
He had lied.
A teacher.
And Miss Smith as well.
Another teacher.
Both of them.
And not just any old lie,
not just a little lie,
but a great, huge lie!

The mother of all lies!
A cup-winning, double-top, heavyweight
championship lie!

Luke had lied often enough.
He was good at it.
But that was all right!
You expected that.
But not a teacher.

It wasn't fair!
It was against the rules!

Luke felt helpless and angry.
He looked up at the posters on the wall.

He read, *"As ye shall sow, so shall ye reap!"*
And *"Those that live by the sword,*
shall die by the sword!"